IMAGES
of America

SLOVAK PITTSBURGH

Slovaks carried on their customs and traditions once they settled in America. Here smiling Slovak men, women, and children pose in costume around 1939 during the celebration of Slovak Day at Kennywood Park in West Mifflin. (Regina Feryok.)

On the cover: Please see page 100. (Teresa Sinchak.)

IMAGES
of America

SLOVAK PITTSBURGH

Lisa A. Alzo

ARCADIA
PUBLISHING

Published by Arcadia Publishing
Charleston, South Carolina

Library of Congress Catalog Card Number: 2006928980

For all general information contact Arcadia Publishing at:
Telephone 843-853-2070
Fax 843-853-0044
E-mail sales@arcadiapublishing.com
For customer service and orders:
Toll-Free 1-888-313-2665

Visit us on the Internet at www.arcadiapublishing.com

To my parents, John and Anna Figlar Alzo, your physical presence in my life is missed every day. And to all of my Slovak ancestors, thank you for making me who I am. This book is for you.

CONTENTS

ACKNOWLEDGMENTS

Slovaks are historically known for their generosity and hospitality. I found this to be especially true for all the wonderful folks I interacted with during the course of my research for this project.

I would like to thank all of those who made this book possible through their donations of historic photographs: Joseph Bielecki; Daniel J. Burns; Sabra Clark; Joanne Engel; Barbara Felak; Regina Feryok; Laurel Figlar; Luanne Francesangeli; Joyce Candi Grove; Diana Hepner; Emily Ivak; George Klempay; Helen Lizanov; Jim Matthias; John Matviya; Karen Mesaros; Arlene, Irene, and Nancy Patuc; James Pelikan; Cathy Schoderbek; Joseph and Albina Senko; Teresa Sinchak; Scarlett Skarupski; Robert Sloss; Susanna Swade; Pavel Tyrpak; William Wassel; and the Abbott, Augenstein, Figlar, and Lizanov families. Thank you for sharing your images and memories.

I extend a deep appreciation to the following photographers, organizations, and societies: Lewis Hine; Holy Trinity Roman Catholic Church; Mifflin Township Historical Society; Monessen Historical Society; SS. Peter and Paul Church; Slovak Radio Hour on WPIT, particularly Rudy and Susan Ondrejco; University of Pittsburgh Slavic Languages Department, especially Prof. Martin Votruba and Christine Metil; Western Pennsylvania Slovak Cultural Association; Western Pennsylvania Slovak Day Committee; and anyone else I may have inadvertently overlooked.

I also wish to thank my editor at Arcadia Publishing, Erin Vosgien, for embracing this project and expertly guiding the writing during the editorial process.

To my grandparents, John and Elizabeth Fenscak Alzo and John and Verona Straka Figlar, and the countless other Slovak immigrants who settled in Pittsburgh and whose hard work and dedication built so many strong and vibrant Slovak "cluster communities," those who have come after are forever in your debt. To my family, I am grateful for your faithful support of all of my writing endeavors.

Finally, to my husband, Michael, thank you for everything (and especially for recovering my computer's hard drive at the critical hour!). Remember, "Happiness is being married to a Slovak!"

The following works are referenced in this book:

Alexander, June Granatir. "Slovak Americans." www.everyculture.com.
Alzo, Lisa A. *Three Slovak Women*, Baltimore: Gateway Press, 2001.
Bell, Thomas. *Out of This Furnace*, Pittsburgh: University of Pittsburgh Press, 1941.
"Population: General Report and Analytical Tables." Vol. II, *The Fourteenth Census of the United States, Taken in the Year 1920*. Washington, 1922.
Senko, Joseph T. *Slovaks in Metropolitan Pittsburgh*, Western Pennsylvania Slovak Cultural Association, 2006.

INTRODUCTION

No other city in the United States is home to more Slovaks than Pittsburgh.

According to the 2000 Federal Census, there were 797,764 people of Slovak heritage living in the United States. Pennsylvania ranked first of the 50 states, with 243,009 (30.5 percent) of these residents, with approximately half living in western Pennsylvania. Within the state, metropolitan Pittsburgh had 105,525 people of Slovak heritage (or 4.5 percent of the city population). This makes greater Pittsburgh the area with the most people of Slovak heritage in the world outside of Slovakia.

Slovak immigrants settled in the Pittsburgh region in the 1890s. It is estimated that close to 100,000 came looking for work and a chance for a better life. The newcomers were lured by the hills and valleys of this new land that reminded them of the farms, forests, and mountains they left behind. They lived in neighborhoods close to their work. Slovaks formed numerous cluster communities throughout western Pennsylvania in such towns as Braddock, Duquesne, Homestead, Munhall, the North Side, Rankin, and Swissvale.

A number of individuals whose parents, grandparents, or great-grandparents were born in Slovakia achieved fame or stature in the arts, athletics, politics, and other fields. These notables are Thomas Bell (novelist), George Blanda (football player), Joseph Gaydos (U.S. Congressman), and Andy Warhol (pop artist), among others. The famous Pittsburgh Slovaks deserve much credit and admiration for their respective accomplishments, but their images and stories have been captured and preserved in countless other published works. Therefore, the faces of the common, everyday Slovak folk grace the pages of this book.

The most difficult part of writing was the selection of photographs. Unfortunately, there were some additional images I had hoped to include but were regretfully unavailable in time to meet the publication deadline. Even so, with the more than 200 images eventually selected, *Slovak Pittsburgh* celebrates the lives of those Slovaks who settled in greater Pittsburgh and the rich heritage that is their legacy.

One

OLD COUNTRY, NEW WORLD

About 620,000 Slovaks came to the United States between 1875 and 1914. Some emigrated for economic reasons, others to escape political repression. The majority of the immigrants to the United States arrived before World War I.

The Industrial Revolution that commenced in the United States in the mid-1800s created huge employment opportunities. At around the same time, the people of Slovakia (which was part of the Austro-Hungarian Empire) were experiencing high unemployment along with political and religious persecution.

During the early part of the 19th century, the Slovak economy grew slowly due to worldwide economic slumps and also because the Industrial Revolution arrived later to Slovakia than to Western Europe and the Czech lands. Thus the Czech lands were more advanced and industrialized, while Slovakia remained an area primarily based on agriculture. As a result, Slovak immigration to the United States increased rapidly at the end of the 19th century as many Slovaks became more and more dissatisfied with local conditions. By 1900, Slovakia had lost over 300,000 of its inhabitants to emigration.

When World War I ended in 1918, so did the 1,000-year reign of the Austro-Hungarian Empire. Consequently, a great migration began out of Slovakia and lasted until 1920. During those years, approximately one million Slovaks came to America.

Many Slovaks returned home after earning enough money to buy land there, but eventually some 500,000 Slovaks settled permanently in the New World. In doing so, many of them left behind family, friends, and neighbors whom they would perhaps never see again.

Slovaks gravitated to areas where industries were expanding and the need for skilled labor was high. More than half the Slovak immigrants went to Pennsylvania and primarily to the mill towns and coal mining districts in the state's western region (hence the large number who settled in Pittsburgh). Other populations inhabited Ohio, New Jersey, New York, and Illinois. Slovaks typically "chain migrated," meaning that they went to places where previous Slovak immigrants already lived.

Slovakia is a landlocked country located at the crossroads between eastern and western Europe. It is bordered by Poland to the north, Hungary to the south, the Czech Republic to the west, and Ukraine to the east. Although Slovakia is a small country with a land mass of 18,919 square miles, its topography varies widely from rugged mountains to dense forests to low, fertile plains. The vast Carpathian Mountain Range stretching along Slovakia's northern border also reaches the central part, where the beautiful Tatras caps the Carpathian system with altitudes as high as 8,711 feet. (Albina Senko.)

This photograph shows a scene from Milpos, a small village located in Saris County in eastern Slovakia. Like other such communities, Milpos consisted mainly of farmland, 15 to 20 homes, and a small church. Its inhabitants came from peasant backgrounds and historically from a feudal society. It was not until 1848, during the time of the Hungarian Revolution, that feudalism was finally abolished. Slovak immigrants who came to the hills and valleys of western Pennsylvania were undoubtedly reminded of the landscape they had left behind. (Emily Ivak.)

Young Slovak women learned how to work from watching their mothers. Typically she would rise early each morning to go out and work in the fields. She would gather the wheat, which had to be ground by hand through a mill in order to make the flour used to bake bread. In addition, young girls learned basic housekeeping duties from their mothers, including cooking, cleaning, sewing, weaving, and dressmaking. She had to be skilled in all aspects of caring for a home so that she would be prepared for marriage. With such long and tedious work, it is no wonder that in those days the Slovak mother was considered an old woman by the time her eldest daughter got married. This photograph of Maria Verbovsky Straka, taken around 1922, shows the reflection of a woman much older than she actually was at the time. Straka looks as though she has endured life, but not enjoyed it. (Lisa A. Alzo.)

Some mothers like the one in this undated photograph had to say goodbye to several, or all, of their children. A deep faith in God helped them cope. (Albina Senko.)

Margaret Strisovska Kolodzej, shown here about 1937, married William Kolodzej in 1935.

Katrina Makovska dons a lovely white dress for this undated photograph. (Albina Senko.)

The traditional Slovak family was patriarchal in nature. Women were forced into the background by cultural and societal barriers, while at the same time acting as the heart and soul of the family. Immigration was a disruptive process for the traditional Slovak family like the one seen here. (Albina Senko.)

In Slovakia, families were often extended, with parents, grandparents, children, aunts, uncles, cousins, and in-laws living under one roof. Three generations of the Figlyar family in Osturna, Slovakia, are pictured around 1906. (Lisa A. Alzo.)

A strong devotion to family is something Slovak immigrants carried with them to the New World. In this undated photograph, a Slovak family is captured wearing its customary ethnic folk dress. (Cathy Schoderbek.)

The war and previous mass emigration depleted many of the small Slovak villages of young, single men. This left young women such as Lizzie and Anna Fenscak (left), shown here around 1913, with slim chances of finding a husband. (Cathy Schoderbek.)

A large number of young Slovak men fled their homeland to escape induction into the Austro-Hungarian military, especially in the years leading up to World War I. It was compulsory for all young men to enlist when they reached the age of 21. This c. 1900s photograph shows three unidentified soldiers who served their time in the army. (Cathy Schoderbek.)

With the end of feudalism, those peasants who found themselves landless were left with few prospects for employment. The Hungarian rulers, who did little to remedy the situation, failed to embrace industrialization, which may have helped ease this problem. The lack of employment, combined with cholera, trachoma, tuberculosis, and typhus epidemics during the 1850s and a series of crop failures and droughts in the 1860s, contributed to the already poor living conditions. Slovaks began to look outside the country for employment opportunities; not long afterward, the great migrations began. America was especially appealing. However, some Slovaks chose to stay behind. This early-1900s photograph shows the blessing of a bell in front of a church in Slovenska Ves. (Albina Senko.)

When immigrants left on the journey to America, it was often common practice for the entire village to gather in celebration and bid farewell to the person leaving. Family and friends met in the center of town and said prayers for a safe journey. Here villagers gather in Osturna, Slovakia, about 1921. Janos Figlyar is standing at the front, to the far left. (Lisa A. Alzo.)

16

Due to the boom of industrialization, America needed strong men to work in its factories, mines, and mills. Steamship agents enticed many laborers from Slovakia by telling marvelous stories, through handbills and newspapers, of how America was a land of plenty, where higher wages and economic and social advantage awaited those who came to its shores. During the early immigration years, Slovak men went to America alone. They typically did not take their wives and children, since most went to earn money and then planned to return to Slovakia to buy land. The wife would remain in the old country to tend to the land and raise the children. Later on, the men would instead establish quarters in America and send for the women and children. William Kolodzej (right), who was born in Donora in 1912, moved back to Slovakia in 1921 but later returned to America in June 1936. (Albina Senko.)

Some Slovak men like Janos Figlyar, pictured here around 1921, were single when they arrived in America—and anxious to find a bride. Figlyar desired a wife from the old country instead of one already settled into American culture. His friend and coworker John Kolcun helped arrange a meeting with, and subsequent marriage to, Verona Straka, his wife's youngest sister. (Lisa A. Alzo.)

By the last two decades of the 19th century, women had the task of shepherding their families to the New World. After 1900, with the population of single young men depleted, the number of marriages declined in Slovakia. After World War I, Slovak women eventually began to follow the pattern set by the Irish of sending single women over to America to establish a home. This photograph of two young Slovak women, Verona Straka (left) and her niece Mary Straka, was taken prior to their departure from Milpos, Slovakia, in 1922. (Lisa A. Alzo.)

Immigrants travel to America on the *Aquitania* on July 26, 1929. The Ragan family, which eventually settled in the steel town of Duquesne, poses with the ship's captain and numerous other unidentified passengers. Included in this picture are the following: (first row) John and Andrew Ragan; (second row) Teresa Ragan holding Paul Ragan; (third row) Jan Ragan, third from left. (Jim Matthias.)

The journey to the New World was an arduous one, as depicted in this 1905 photograph of a Slovak immigrant woman at Ellis Island. (Lewis Hine.)

Two

RODINA

After religion, *rodina* (family) was next in importance to the Slovak people. Families were often extended. In the old country, parents, grandparents, children, aunts, uncles, cousins, and in-laws lived under one roof.

The traditional Slovak family was patriarchal in nature. Women were forced into the background by cultural and societal barriers, yet one should not underestimate the importance of the Slovak wives and mothers. They were often the "silent glue" that held their families together, at times simultaneously assuming the roles of caretaker, nurturer, financial manager, and disciplinarian.

A strong devotion to family is something Slovak immigrants carried with them to the New World, and they strived to teach their children and grandchildren some key life lessons, including the need for family solidarity, a deep religious faith, the benefits of working hard, and the importance of preserving the continuity of the ethnic tradition.

This 1921 photograph of the Klempays reflects the typical close-knit Slovak family. Pictured here, from left to right, are the following: (first row) Julia, Joseph Klempay, Mrs. Klempay, Charles, Francis, and Ray (very front); (second row) Anna (later Sister Blanche), Andrew, Alexander, John, Paul, and Mary. This was taken a short time before Anna left to enter the Ursuline Community. (George Klempay.)

Anna Drevenak Dzumela stands in German Square in this undated photograph. (Diana Hepner.)

In this undated family photograph, Joseph Dzumela and his daughter Mary stand side by side. (Diana Hepner.)

This 1918 family portrait of the Sinchak family includes, from left to right, Steven, Anna, Michael, and Stanley. (Teresa Sinchak.)

Anna Tomascovic Sinchak, her husband, Michael Sinchak, and sons Stanley (left) and Steven pose with an American flag in this patriotic photograph taken in 1916 in Monessen. (Teresa Sinchak.)

Michael Hanyak, a member of Holy Trinity Parish in Duquesne, is seen in an undated photograph. (Joanne Engel.)

Ann Hanyak (left), one of 10 children, poses with her mother, Anna. (Joanne Engel.)

This undated photograph shows Michael Gajdos of SS. Peter and Paul Church in Duquesne. (Joanne Engel.)

Theresa Sersen (left) and her sister-in-law Mary Gajdos immigrated to the United States together. This undated photograph was taken at *Odpust* (banquet) at Mount St. Mucrina in Uniontown on Labor Day. *Odpust* is a celebration of pastoral, religious, and parish activities. It usually involved a mass and festival. (Joanne Engel.)

In this 1909 image, Mihal Skarupa (left) poses with his brother Jan in Bulger, where they worked in the coal mines. (William Wassel.)

Mihal Skarupa is shown with his children in Bulger in 1909. (William Wassel.)

Mihal Skarupa is seen here with his family around 1938 in the Turtle Creek area. (William Wassel.)

The Matviya family of Blairsville gathers for a c. 1922 portrait. Pictured here, from left to right, are the following: (first row) Anna, Andy Jr., Andy Sr., Mary (mother), and Mary (daughter); (second row) Mickey and Mike. (John Matviya.)

This photograph of the Klempay family was taken sometime in 1904 during the moves from Bolivar or the vicinity, West Fairfield Township near Johnstown, to Youngstown, Ohio, and then six months later to East Palestine, Ohio. The family then traveled back to Youngstown on September 19, 1919. (George Klempay.)

Although Slovaks typically maintained a close-knit family system, by the mid-20th century, Slovak Americans were moving from the cities to the suburbs. The Klempays, shown here about 1914, were ahead of this trend as they left western Pennsylvania for East Palestine, Ohio, a bit earlier. (George Klempay.)

Depicted here is a typical large Slovak Catholic family. This photograph was taken around 1921 in East Palestine, Ohio, a locale not far from Pittsburgh. (George Klempay.)

The Patuc family poses in 1923. From left to right are Joe, John, Anna (holding Steve), Frank, and Mike. (Arlene, Irene, and Nancy Patuc.)

Mary Balun Bednar, at age 50, sits on the porch of her Duquesne home. (Robert M. Sloss Jr.)

A close-up of Mary Kochis Matviya in babushka, hard at work in Bairdstown, is captured in this c. 1940s photograph. (John Matviya.)

John Alzo, smartly dressed in a suit, poses with his wife, Elizabeth, and his young daughter Anna, also finely attired, around the 1920s.

This undated photograph shows John and Mary Hatala with their two young children. (Cathy Schoderbek.)

The Ragan children gather for a photograph around 1938–1939. From left to right are Anna, Teresa, Albert, Mary, Paul, John, and Andy. (Jim Matthias.)

In this c. 1943 image, Teresa and Jan Ragan (far right) and their children pose with Rev. John Kerchnak, pastor of Holy Trinity Roman Catholic Church, Duquesne, from 1914 to 1955. (Jim Matthias.)

It was common for Slovak families to take group portraits, as evidenced by this Yanichko family photograph. (Robert M. Sloss Jr.)

A typical mill family is shown in front of the home on West Thirteenth Avenue in Homestead in 1943. Pictured here, from left to right, are the following: (first row) Michael Sinchak, Frances Harman, Mary Ann Sinchak, and Audrey Harman; (second row) Mary (Harman) Sinchak, Michael Harman, Andrew Harman, and Susan Harman. (Teresa Sinchak.)

These two unidentified young men look mischievous in their suits and hats. (Cathy Schoderbek.)

Irene Vadas and Lou Pelikan, shown on Labor Day in 1939, were married in 1942. (James Pelikan.)

Photographs such as this one of six-month-old Anna Alzo, taken in 1918, were true family treasures. (Lisa A. Alzo.)

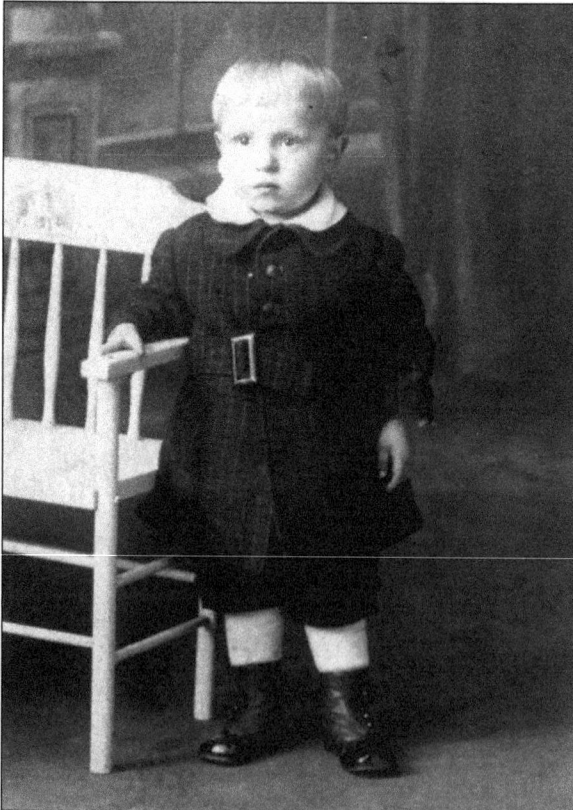

In this undated photograph, an impeccably dressed young John Fenchak holds on to a chair but does not smile for the camera.

A young John Frena, wearing a cap and knickers, is all smiles in this undated photograph. (Cathy Schoderbek.)

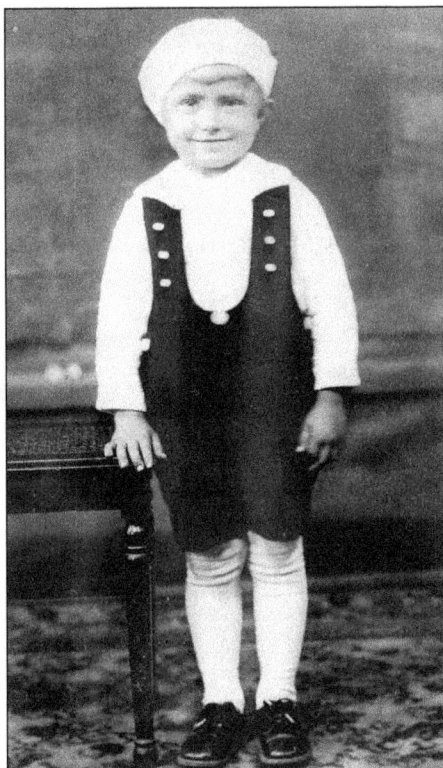

Vincent Salva shares a happy moment with his daughter Sabra around 1938. (Sabra Clark.)

John Figlar is dressed in his Sunday best for this photograph taken in front of his home on Hill Street in Duquesne. (Helen Lizanov.)

John Alzo Sr., seen here at age 42, recovers from an operation at his Duquesne home in 1936. The look on his face is one of engagement; he is looking at the camera as if to say, "Come, sit down and talk with me." (Lisa A. Alzo.)

Several members of the Hatala family take a moment to pose for this undated photograph taken during a gathering outdoors. (Cathy Schoderbek.)

Proud father John Kolcun poses on the porch of his home with four of his children. (Lisa A. Alzo.)

In this casual, undated photograph, Mary and John Frena stand arm in arm near their Duquesne residence. (Cathy Schoderbek.)

Stanley and Mary Sinchak are dressed in traditional Slovak costume for Slovak Day in Kennywood Park in 1938. (Teresa Sinchak.)

Anna and George Bavolar pose for a photograph before going to church in the 1940s. (Cathy Schoderbek.)

Slovaks stayed close with family even as children grew up, and perhaps moved away. Here the adult children in the Ragan family of Duquesne are seen with their mother. (Jim Matthias.)

Frank J. Pustinger Sr. (first row, second from left) and Julia Pustinger (first row, center) are pictured with sons Stephen Pustinger (second row, far left) and Alexander P. Pustinger (second row, second from left), along with a few other unidentified family members. Alexander was an undertaker who is mentioned in Thomas Bell's 1941 novel *Out of This Furnace*. An unidentified female family member who had previously passed away is superimposed into the photograph at the back. (Susanna Swade.)

Three

FROM CRADLE TO GRAVE

Slovaks celebrated life at every stage. In particular, weddings, births, and funerals were the three most special occasions in the Slavic community. These life events also took on a deeper meaning for those involved because of the direct correlation to sacraments in the church, namely christening, marriage, and extreme unction (anointing of the sick or last rites). Such religious feast days represented the expansion (or loss, in the case of death) of both the immediate family and the larger parish or church family and involved some type of gathering.

In America, Slovaks often documented these major life events through photographs. Sometimes they borrowed a camera from relatives, friends, or neighbors. Other times, since money was tight for most Slovak families, they sacrificed in order to afford a photographer for a wedding ceremony, the arrival of a new son or daughter, or to preserve the eternal memory of a deceased loved one.

Elizabeth Alzo holds her infant daughter Anna in front of her home around 1919. (Lisa A. Alzo.)

Three unidentified children are dressed in their Sunday best for this undated photograph. (Cathy Schoderbek.)

In Slovakia, weddings were lengthy affairs that, depending on the village's size, could involve nearly all of the inhabitants. Preparatory rituals for the marriage, the ceremony, and the subsequent celebrations could last a week. This unidentified Slovak couple is surrounded by a large number of folks—men, women, and children—who are most likely family, close friends, or neighbors joining in the celebration. (Cathy Schoderbek.)

An unidentified Slovak bride and groom are pictured on their wedding day. As was customary during the festivities following the ceremony, the bride's veil would be removed and replaced with a *cepec*, a bonnet or cap, to signify her acceptance as a married woman. (Cathy Schoderbek.)

45

Joseph and Juliana Masurak Klempay married on May 30, 1891. Both were born in Slovakia, came to the United States through New York, settled in western Pennsylvania, and later moved to Youngstown, Ohio. Notice the bride's dark wedding dress. (George Klempay.)

This *c.* 1900 photograph shows Vasil Yanichko and Helena Mackuscin on their wedding day. The ceremony was held at SS. Peter and Paul Byzantine Catholic Church in Duquesne. (Robert M. Sloss Jr.)

46

Here Mary Troychak and John Jurenek pose happily with their unidentified bridal attendants. Marriage patterns influenced family and community dynamics. For the immigrant generation, the norm was marriage between Slovaks.

Traditional Slovak wedding ceremonies were complex affairs. Weddings began with a solemn church service and ended with a large reception, usually held in a local hall to accommodate the several hundred guests. The celebration could last from two days to two weeks, depending on how much money the bride's parents were willing, or able, to spend. In Slovakia, a typical wedding lasted as long as 10 days. In America, the economic and social conditions did not permit such lengthy celebrations. This undated photograph depicts the wedding of Zella Gergel and John Janosik. (Barbara Felak.)

Immigrant women often had a difficult time adjusting to their new lives in America. One of the ways to help alleviate some of the problems, especially loneliness, was through marriage. Single Slovak women were good candidates for matchmaking with single immigrant men. Often a woman could not choose whom she married. Mary Straka (right) is pictured on her wedding day in 1924. She was matched in marriage to a steelworker named Andrew Yuhasz (Juhász), a boarder who lived in her mother's house. Mary's aunt Verona Straka (left) served as the maid of honor. (Lisa A. Alzo.)

This photograph of Mary Matviya and Jim Yuzawich was taken on their wedding day, September 11, 1937. (John Matviya.)

Slovak weddings were large, joyous occasions celebrated with food, drink, and dancing. The festivities often lasted as long as three days. Janos and Verona Straka Figlar married in 1924. The 31 people in this wedding day photograph—all dressed in their Sunday best—included relatives, friends, and several of Janos's coworkers and their wives. Verona first immigrated to Duquesne in 1892, and although she and Janos were married in Barton, Ohio, the couple eventually moved back to Duquesne in the 1930s and settled there permanently. (Lisa A. Alzo.)

Joseph Yaniga and Mary Kupetski married in Fairchance on May 21, 1919. (Arlene, Irene, and Nancy Patuc.)

This wedding photograph of Frank Patuc and Anna Maurer was taken on October 13, 1923, in Brier Hill. (Arlene, Irene, and Nancy Patuc.)

The wedding party gathers for a photograph at the marriage of Joseph Yaniga and Mary Kupetski on May 21, 1919, in Fairchance. (Arlene, Irene, and Nancy Patuc.)

This undated photograph depicts a double wedding. The grooms, Joe and Julius Chovan of Monessen, and their respective brides, Mary and Anna Kerestes, are shown with their wedding parties. (Barbara Felak.)

This photograph was taken at the wedding of Ann Varga and John Gogol. (Barbara Felak.)

Joe Janosik and Anna Molnar are shown here on their wedding day.

The marriage of Irene Pettko and Emil Forgac is documented in this undated photograph. (Barbara Felak.)

Margaret and John Novak and their family are photographed on the couple's wedding day. (Barbara Felak.)

William Kolodzej and Margaret Strisovska were married in 1935 in Slovakia. William, who was born in Pittsburgh, returned there in 1936, leaving his wife and four-week-old daughter, Albina. Because of World War II, the family remained separated until 1946. (Albina Senko.)

This photograph of John and Mary (Stropkay) Senko was taken at their 1914 wedding in Pittsburgh. (Joseph Senko.)

Andrew and Susan Harman pose in Homestead on their wedding day in 1914. (Teresa Sinchak.)

Mary Balun and John Bednar were married around 1915 in St. Mary's Byzantine Greek Catholic Church in Trauger. St. Mary's Greek Catholic Church was founded on January 1, 1894, under the leadership of Rev. Stephen Dzubay. (Robert M. Sloss Jr.)

A typical Slovak immigrant couple celebrates the wedding day. The bride is wearing a traditional dress and veil. This photograph of Janos Alsio and Erzebet (Elizabeth) Fenscak was taken on January 21, 1915. Janos (who later changed his name to John Alzo) was born on January 1, 1894, in Kucsin, Hungary (later Slovakia), and arrived at Ellis Island on October 29, 1910. Erzebet was born on February 10, 1897, in Posa, Hungary (later Slovakia), and disembarked at Ellis Island on May 14, 1914. (Lisa A. Alzo.)

On October 14, 1947, Anna Figlar became the bride of John Alzo Jr., a fellow Slovak, in SS. Peter and Paul Greek Catholic Church. It was a balmy Tuesday—an unusual day for a wedding by today's standards—but back then it was not uncommon for couples to marry during the week. The wedding was a much-anticipated event, especially for Anna's family, not only because she was the eldest daughter, but also because she was the first of her siblings to marry. (Lisa A. Alzo.)

Slovaks often had photographs taken to mark special occasions in their children's lives. Here an unidentified child dressed in a white outfit and bonnet smiles for a snapshot at Kennywood Park in West Mifflin in May 1950. (Cathy Schoderbek.)

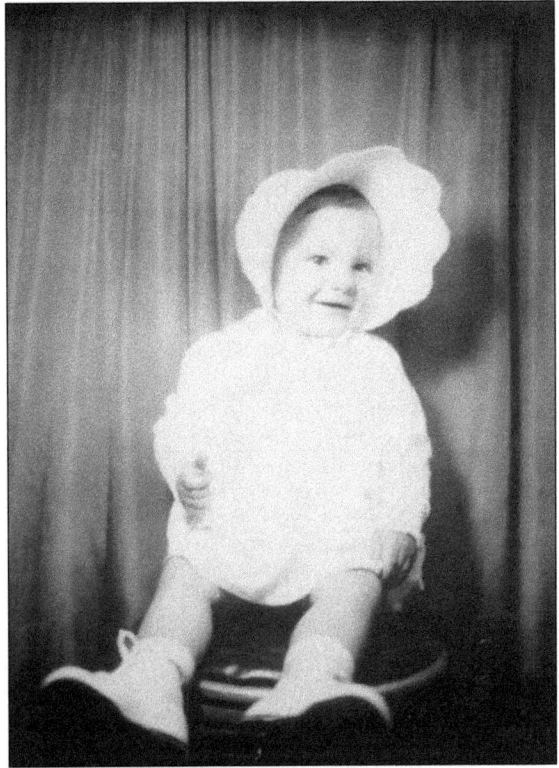

Holiday gatherings at social clubs were one of the many activities enjoyed by Slovaks. In this early-1970s photograph, a young Lisa Alzo sits on Santa's lap to tell him what she wants for Christmas. (Lisa A. Alzo.)

Grave markers bearing Slovak inscriptions, such as this one for Mary Ceyba at Holy Trinity Roman Catholic Church Cemetery in West Mifflin, can be found in any number of cemeteries affiliated with Slovak churches in western Pennsylvania. The inscription translates as, "There rests Mary Ceyba, born 1891." (Lisa A. Alzo.)

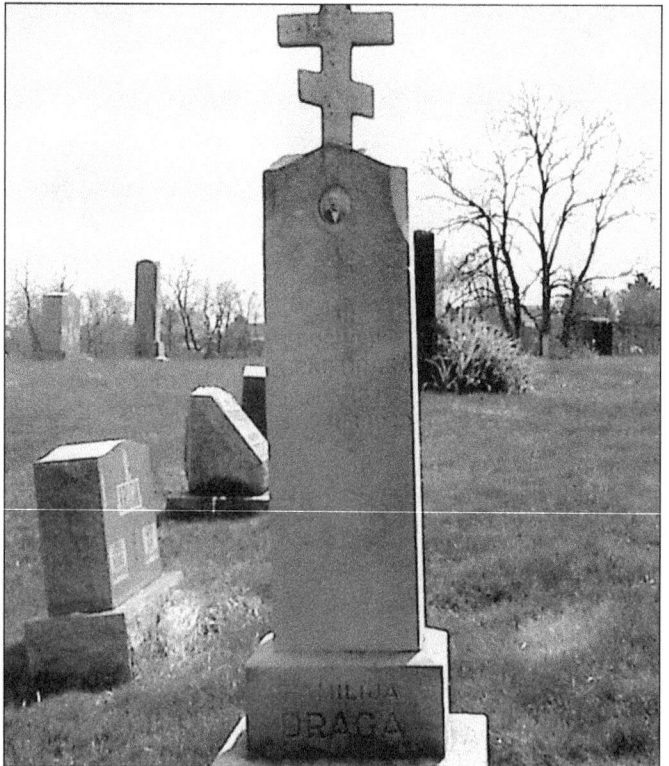

Slovaks often had elaborate grave markers erected for their loved ones. A common practice was to include a photograph of the deceased on the tombstone. (Lisa A. Alzo.)

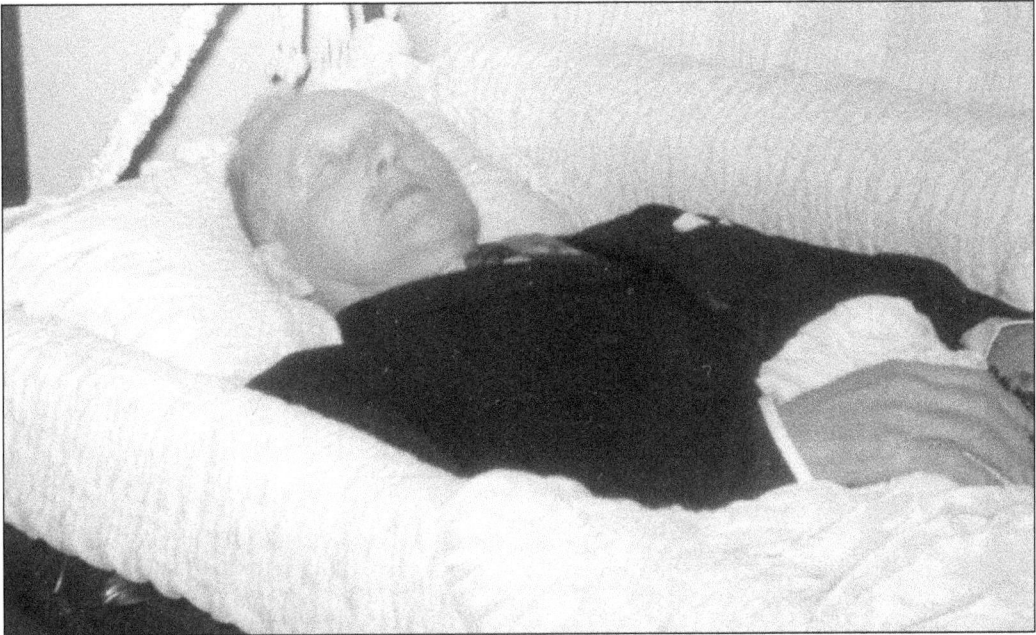

Proper burial of the dead was a ritual that spanned several days. This photograph of John Alzo Sr. was taken at his funeral in 1962. John died of a heart attack at age 67. Ironically, earlier in the day he had served as a pallbearer at the funeral of one of his friends. (Lisa A. Alzo.)

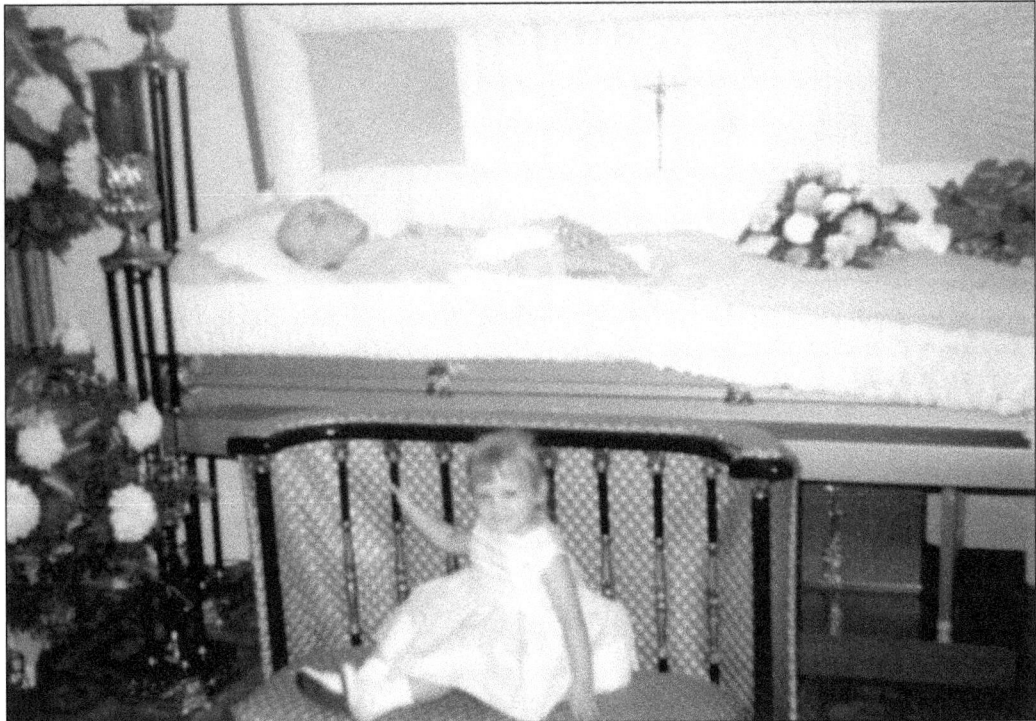

The concept of family carried through even during the death of a loved one. Children were included, and often photographs were taken with the deceased. Lisa Alzo is shown in front of the coffin holding the body of her paternal grandmother, Elizabeth, in 1966. (Lisa A. Alzo.)

Family and friends of Duquesne resident Michael Sivak pose with the deceased at the time of his burial in 1919 in SS. Peter and Paul Cemetery. The priest and church cantor can also be seen. Memorial photography was a popular way to honor the deceased in the late 19th and early 20th centuries. Deaths also triggered a host of superstitions. Immediately following a person's demise, Slovaks covered all the mirrors and closed all the windows in his home. They believed that these measures would prevent the dead from returning. (Lisa A. Alzo.)

Four

RELIGION

For Slovaks, religion has been above all in importance since the time Christianity was brought to the area (then known as Great Moravia) in 863 A.D. by two Byzantine monks, Cyril and Methodius, who eventually became known as the Apostles to the Slavs. Over the course of the next several centuries, grand churches of various faiths, Roman or Greek Catholic, Orthodox, and Evangelical Lutheran, began to develop in villages throughout Slovakia.

Early Slovak immigrants included Catholics, Lutherans, and Calvinists, but the majority were Roman Catholic. Lutherans comprised the second-largest body of Slovak immigrants. Slovak Byzantine rite Catholics also migrated to the United States and organized a few churches, but more often they cooperated with other Byzantine rite Catholics, especially Carpatho-Rusyns, to found ethnically mixed parishes. Disagreements surrounding the fact that Byzantine rite clergyman could marry while Roman Catholic priests could not became a significant cause for difference between the two faiths in the United States. As a result, some Byzantine rite Catholic Slovaks then joined the Orthodox church. Only a small number of Slovak Calvinists immigrated to the United States.

By 1920, there were about 28 Catholic Slovak churches in Pittsburgh, many with adjoining schools and social halls built in Slovak neighborhoods. The Slovak Lutherans and Byzantine or Greek Catholics also founded their own churches and organizations. In general, Slovak churches survived for decades as ethnic institutions, but unfortunately were not immune to change. In Pittsburgh, like other comparable cities and towns where Slovaks settled, as the immigrant generation died and their descendants moved out of ethnic neighborhoods, some Slovak churches saw their membership decline, while others closed or were taken over by new immigrant groups. However, a number of vibrant Slovak Lutheran and Catholic churches still exist.

Saints Cyril and Methodius

V každej slovenskej osade bola obetovaná sv. Omša
k úcte Svv. Cyrilla a Methoda.

This drawing depicts SS. Cyril and Methodius, two Byzantine monks who eventually became known as the Apostles to the Slavs because they brought Christianity to the area of present-day Slovakia in 863 A.D.

The interior of St. Mary's Greek Catholic Church, Bradenville, is pictured around 1918. St. Mary's was founded in 1905. (John Matviya.)

Andrej and Mary Matviya donated this stained-glass window, pictured in 1980, to St. Mary's Greek Catholic Church in Bradenville. Due to remodeling and renovation in the early 1990s, the church eventually replaced all of its stained-glass windows. This one appropriately found its way to the kitchen of John and Mary's grandson John Matviya of New Alexandria. (John Matviya.)

Fr. Nicholas Hodobay became the first pastor of Holy Trinity Roman Catholic Church on September 18, 1902. The first frame church was erected on South First Street before the end of 1901, and additions were constructed as the congregation grew. After internal controversy over additional building, and the subsequent departure of Father Hodobay, the brick building was finally completed in 1905. The church was eventually moved to a site on Grant Avenue Extension in West Mifflin. The cornerstone blessing and the laying ceremony were held on August 24, 1969, and the first Sunday mass was offered on April 26, 1970. Holy Trinity Church still has an active congregation that strives to maintain its ethnic Slovak ties. (Daniel J. Burns.)

This photograph of the altar in the Holy Trinity Roman Catholic Church Convent in Duquesne was taken in the 1940s. Morgan and Company of Homestead commenced construction on the convent in March 1926. The final cost was $32,890.56. The Incarnate Word Sisters from Victoria, Texas, came to teach the children and reside in the convent. The Incarnate Word Sisters taught at the school from 1908 until about 1944, followed by the Vincentian Sisters of Charity from Perrysville. (Cathy Schoderbek.)

This modern photograph shows the front of St. Paul Evalengelical Lutheran Church in Braddock. This parish was one of a number of vibrant Slovak Lutheran churches that formed throughout western Pennsylvania and the United States. (Joseph Bielecki.)

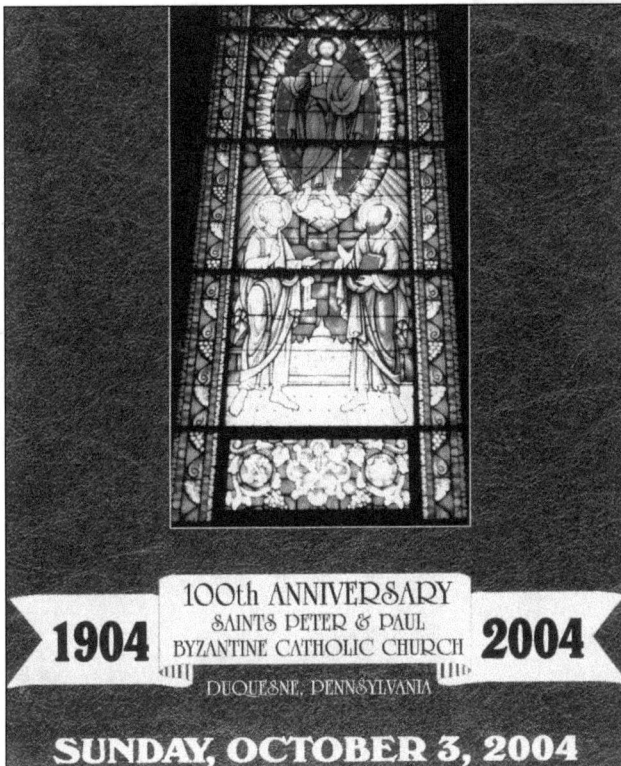

100th ANNIVERSARY
SAINTS PETER & PAUL
BYZANTINE CATHOLIC CHURCH
DUQUESNE, PENNSYLVANIA
1904   2004

SUNDAY, OCTOBER 3, 2004

Slovak churches in Pittsburgh survived for decades as ethnic institutions. In 2004, SS. Peter and Paul Byzantine Catholic Church celebrated its 100th anniversary. (SS. Peter and Paul Byzantine Catholic Church.)

Sr. Mary Camilla, shown here in the 1930s, was one of many Slovaks who went into religious service. (Cathy Schoderbek.)

Having a priest in the family was an honor. In this undated photograph, Fr. Michael Bodnar poses with several proud family members. (Scarlett Skarupski.)

This 1921 photograph depicts Rev. John Pavlik, pastor of SS. Peter and Paul Byzantine Catholic Church, with his faithful stewards—his church committee. (SS. Peter and Paul Byzantine Catholic Church.)

Parishioners of Slovak Catholic churches were often photographed with their priests, as evidenced by this undated photograph taken in Monessen. (Regina Feryok.)

Johnny Alzo is dressed all in white, with Bible and rosaries in hand, on his First Holy Communion day in 1933. First Holy Communion is an important sacrament in the Roman Catholic Church and a joyous occasion for Slovak Catholic families. (Lisa A. Alzo.)

Ann (left) and Mary Balint are angelic in their white dresses on their First Holy Communion day in the 1940s. (Cathy Schoderbek.)

Youngster John Balint, dressed in a white shirt and dark knickers, holds his prayer book open for this *c.* 1940s First Holy Communion image. (Cathy Schoderbek.)

Two unidentified girls stand solemnly for this undated photograph taken on the special occasion of a First Holy Communion. The girl on the left wears a long veil and holds a prayer book and rosary beads. (Cathy Schoderbek.)

The First Holy Communion class from SS. Peter and Paul Church on First Street in Duquesne poses with its cantor, Andrew Hleba (right), and an unidentified priest in this undated photograph. (Joanne Engel.)

Religion was an important aspect of the lives of Slovak immigrants. Here 27 boys and girls dressed in fine white attire for their First Communion day pose with Sr. Mary Camilla in front of Holy Trinity Catholic School in Duquesne on June 5, 1941. (Cathy Schoderbek.)

In this undated photograph, a group of Slovaks can be seen in devotional prayer near a statue of the Blessed Virgin Mary during *Odpust* in Uniontown. (Cathy Schoderbek.)

Religious celebrations were a major part of daily life for Slovaks. Parishioners from Holy Trinity Roman Catholic Church in Duquesne file in procession from their school and convent en route to the church to celebrate a feast day of the Blessed Virgin Mary. (Cathy Schoderbek.)

Michael Sinchak, president of the Slovak Catholic Federation, places the marble stone containing the relics of St. Cyril in the new altar restored by the federation in the Basilica of St. Clement in Rome during the Holy Year pilgrimage of 1950. (Teresa Sinchak.)

Michael Sinchak arranged tours to Europe that included visits with Pope Pius XII, as seen in this 1952 photograph. (Teresa Sinchak.)

Five

EDUCATION

For immigrants in general, the matter of education was a new concept. In America, education was compulsory and involved a choice between public and parochial schooling. Many Slavic parents viewed the public school as an enemy, objecting to what they presumed was an emphasis on materialism, "American ways," and anti-religious teachings. Immigrant parents also had bitter memories of the public school in Slovakia where Hungarian officials tried to eradicate their culture and turn them into Magyars. Such deep contempt kept some parents from seeing the benefits to be gained through a public education. As a result, many Slovaks were driven to support parochial schools staffed by the priests and nuns of the local ethnic church in an effort to ensure their children received instruction in the values and traditions they cherished. Only those children who attended parochial schools were taught in the Slovak language.

In parochial schools, the day began around 8:00 a.m. with mass, during which children would kneel facing the altar. During the school day, children were taught the same courses as those who went to public school: reading, writing, arithmetic, art, geography, and social studies. On Friday afternoons, however, nuns taught Slovak language, history, and songs. Slovak Greek Catholic children usually attended Greek or Roman Catholic parochial schools or went to public school.

In general, the majority of Slavic immigrants had difficulty accepting the common notion that education opened the way to quick advancement in the world. They believed that in school children learned the necessary skills to survive in society, but that once these were learned it was time to leave.

On June 20, 1923, eight lots belonging to the Carnegie Land Company on South Third and Whitfield Streets in Duquesne were purchased by Holy Trinity Roman Catholic Church at a cost of $9,500 for the purpose of building a new school and convent. Construction of the school began in February 1924. This undated photograph shows the large building, which was constructed with safety in mind and fire-proofed as much as possible for that era. (Cathy Schoderbek.)

Smiling youngsters in the third grade at Holy Trinity School in Duquesne sit attentively in November 1941. (Cathy Schoderbek.)

Unidentified schoolchildren pose with their teacher in front of the school in this undated photograph. (Cathy Schoderbek.)

Taken in 1922, this photograph shows students from Bairdstown No. 13, Room 1, in Westmoreland County. Appearing in the second row, third from the right, is Andy Matviya Jr.; second from the right is John Matviya. (John Matviya.)

Slovak immigrants were extremely proud when their children graduated from high school. Anna Figlar, the first of seven children in her family to graduate, wears a cap and gown at her 1943 graduation from Duquesne High School. (Lisa A. Alzo.)

Irene Vadas is shown in her cap and gown during her 1939 graduation from McKeesport High School. (James Pelikan.)

Sisters Helen and Elizabeth Alzo pose for a photograph upon graduation from high school in Duquesne in 1941. (Lisa A. Alzo.)

John Alzo is pictured with his diploma from Duquesne High School, received in June 1943. Two months later, he would be drafted into service for World War II and join the navy. (Lisa A. Alzo.)

Students from Holy Name School in Monessen, grades one through eight, gather for a c. 1937 photograph. (Regina Feryok.)

The many students of the Holy Trinity School (a Slovak parish) hold diplomas upon their 1935 graduation in McKeesport. (James Pelikan.)

Six

AT WORK

Slovaks were not the owners of the mills, factories, or mines that made Pittsburgh a thriving American city, but through their blood, sweat, and tears, they were a large part of the workforce that kept these industries running. As a result, many Slovaks were victims at the hands of the jobs that put bread on their tables. Numerous accidents in the factories, mills, and mines tragically took the lives of countless Slovak workers at one time or another in just about every community.

The Great Depression struck the Pittsburgh area and its workers hard. Employment and production in the steel industry declined drastically. By 1932, almost one-third of the total workforce was out of work (approximately 12 million people total and about 3 million women).

To make ends meet, Slovak women were sometimes forced to work outside the home, typically as domestics or housekeepers. In addition, the taking in of boarders was a common practice among Slovak women—one of the key means available to earn extra money. The boarders were usually unmarried Slovak men who worked in the mills. As well as giving them a place to sleep, the woman washed her boarders' clothes, prepared their breakfasts of bread and coffee, packed their lunch buckets, and had hot meals waiting for them when they came home after their shifts ended. Many young Slovak women were introduced to their future spouses through family members who ran boardinghouses. With the next generation, women eventually found employment as secretaries or in various positions in local department stores. A few even went to work in factories or at other jobs traditionally held by men (especially during the war years).

In addition to their regular jobs, many Slovaks worked hard at building, cleaning, and repairing their own houses, or at helping relatives and neighbors with such tasks. They also took great pride in using their skills to help build churches and other institutions in their communities.

Some Slovaks who had originally settled in western Pennsylvania eventually headed west and found other employment. The Michael Klempay family moved to Youngstown, Ohio. Here family members stand in front of their tailor shop in 1923. A few years later, Klempay moved to Cambridge Springs to a farm that is still in the family.

John Janosik is shown inside the Monessen grocery store he owned during the Great Depression. (Barbara Felak.)

"I've Been Working on the Railroad" is the theme song for these three unidentified workers repairing the track in this 1970s photograph. (Lisa A. Alzo.)

Stanley Sinchak stands in front of Sinchak's Grocery on Schoonmaker Avenue in Monessen in 1936. (Teresa Sinchak.)

Slovak women worked many hours on household chores. In this 1960s photograph, Elizabeth Alzo poses next to a lace curtain she has hung out to dry on a special frame after washing it by hand in a metal laundry tub. (Lisa A. Alzo.)

John Janosik stands outside of his store, Novak and Janosik Groceries and Meats, with his niece Mary Kovach (far right) and an unidentified woman. In the window is a stack of Heinz ketchup bottles. An unidentified boy appears in the foreground. (Barbara Felak.)

Driven by a strong work ethic, Slovaks labored just as hard to improve the appearance of their own homes as they did in their daily jobs. In this 1970s photograph, John Figlar takes a break from assisting with repairs on his neighbor's house on Hill Street in Duquesne.

John Alzo, in cap and overalls, hammers bricks level using a hammer and spirit level while on the job as a carpenter for the Union Railroad in the 1970s. (Lisa A. Alzo.)

John Janosik, seen here behind his desk, served as city treasurer in Monessen in the early 1940s. (Barbara Felak.)

Some Slovaks opted to start their own businesses. Michael Sinchak poses with his family in front of his real estate and insurance office in Monessen in 1947. (Teresa Sinchak.)

Keeping a clean house was a priority for the Slovak woman. Elizabeth Alzo holds her broom while taking a break from housework in this undated photograph. (Lisa A. Alzo.)

More employment opportunities were available to first-generation Slovak American women than their immigrant mothers. Here Anna Alzo looks up from her desk during a work day at the office of McKeesport optometrist Dr. R. W. Hutton in the 1970s. (Lisa A. Alzo.)

Two workers are ready for shoppers at the Novak and Janosik Groceries and Meats store in Monessen. (Barbara Felak.)

Irene Yaniga (third from left) and her coworkers—Union Supply employees—take a moment to pose for a photograph while on strike in Palmer around 1946. (Arlene, Irene, and Nancy Patuc.)

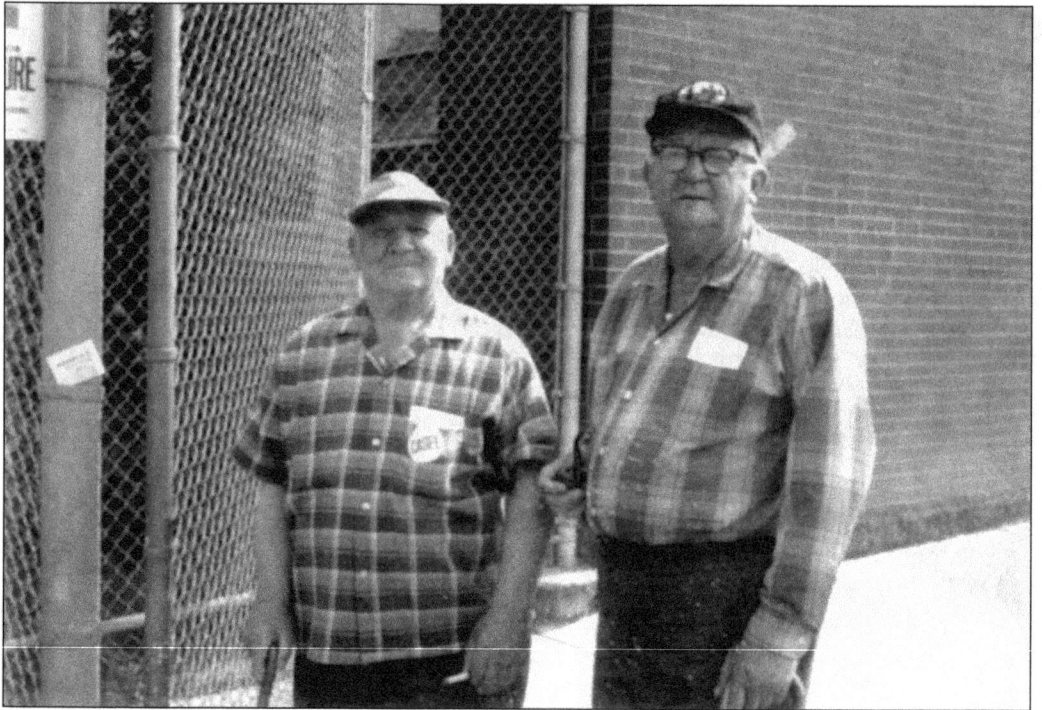

Two longtime steelworkers, John Figlar (left) and Herman Hensler are serious in this 1970s photograph taken in Duquesne. (Lisa A. Alzo.)

Countless numbers of Slovaks lost their jobs when the steel mills in towns throughout the Pittsburgh region shut down operations. This 1991 image shows the remnants of the former United States Steel Works in Duquesne, which officially closed its doors for good in 1984. On one of the buildings inside the plant (not visible) is a telling inscription: "8-25-84 R. I. P." (Lisa A. Alzo.)

Seven

THOSE WHO SERVED

Slovak immigrants and their descendants bravely served the United States during times of conflict, including World War I, World War II, Korea, Vietnam, the Gulf War, and other peacekeeping efforts. Many grandchildren and great-grandchildren of these Slovaks are currently serving in the military. A number of memorials in cities and towns in the greater Pittsburgh area were erected as a tribute to those who gave their lives defending freedom.

Many Slovaks also participated in drill teams and other military-themed organizations associated with their churches or communities.

Three fellow Slovaks and good friends from Duquesne—Andrew Hleba (left), John Alzo (center), and Michael Belich—got together for this 1943 photograph. (Lisa A. Alzo.)

Joseph Figlar (right) and an unidentified army buddy smile for the camera at camp in Hokkaido, Japan, in this undated photograph. (Helen Lizanov.)

While serving in the navy during World War II, John "Pee Wee" Figlar stands at attention in front of the United States flag. (Helen Lizanov.)

Joseph Figlar enlisted in the United States Panama Canal Department of the army. In this undated snapshot, he poses in uniform in front of his Duquesne home. (Helen Lizanov.)

John Alzo was drafted and entered navy service on August 16, 1943. Following boot camp training at Great Lakes, he boarded the USS *Tablerock* on December 15, 1943. Alzo said that when he was drafted he actually got to choose which branch, so he picked the navy. Why? So he "wouldn't have to sleep in a foxhole." In the navy, he would have a bunk. Alzo referred to his days in the service as being on "a floating bomb" because the ship hauled fuel for fighter planes. (Lisa A. Alzo.)

Edward Bavolar looks proud in his navy uniform in December 1941. (Cathy Schoderbek.)

This photograph of Michael Figlar was taken at Fort Meade, Maryland, during his days serving in the army. (Helen Lizanov.)

Nicholas Lizanov served his country in the navy during the Korean War. (Helen Lizanov.)

While on leave from the army in the 1950s, Joseph Figlar (right) and an unidentified buddy pose in front of a car on Crawford Avenue in Duquesne while another unidentified man looks on. (Helen Lizanov.)

Many Slovak families said goodbye to loved ones during times of military conflict. In this c. 1950s photograph, Helen Figlar poses with her brother Michael, who enlisted in the army. (Helen Lizanov.)

Several unidentified soldiers are shown in front of a plane named *The American-Slovak* in this World War II photograph. (Teresa Sinchak.)

Whether naturalized citizens or permanent residents of the United States, a number of Slovak men showed their patriotic spirit, as evidenced by this "drill team" posing for a c. 1914 photograph in Pittsburgh. (Holy Trinity Church.)

This star, created by Pittsburgh artist Karen Mesaros in 2006, honors Sgt. Michael Strank, United States Marine Corps, a Slovak Rusyn immigrant to Franklin Boro (near Johnstown) who gave the command and helped raise the flag atop Mount Suribachi, Iwo Jima, on February 23, 1945. Strank was one of the six men immortalized in the famous photograph taken by Joe Rosenthal. (Karen Mesaros.)

Eight

SLOVAK CLUSTERS

The earlier Slovak immigrants (arriving after 1870 or so) created communities that reflected Old World villages—people who practiced the same religion, spoke the same dialect, enjoyed the same food and music, and felt a kinship that helped them survive harsh living and working conditions, preserve their native culture, and maintain a distinct Slovak identity in North America. These immigrants established churches, schools, fraternal benefit societies, and Slovak organizations that made life easier and adjustment less traumatic.

Their "cluster communities" enabled Slovaks to help each other when any of the families incurred a tragedy. Thus, the formation of fraternal benefit societies began. Several such groups were formed by Slovak activists to help immigrants with their insurance needs and to organize fraternal, social, literary, and cultural programs. There are seven Slovak fraternals still active today, all of which have more members in the greater Pittsburgh area than anywhere else. These include the following: the National Slovak Society (the first fraternal benefit organization in America, founded in Pittsburgh in 1890), the United Lutheran Society (established in 1893), the Ladies Pennsylvania Slovak Catholic Union (founded in 1898), the First Catholic Slovak Union of the United States and Canada (also known as Jednota, formed in Cleveland in 1890 by Fr. Stephen Furdek), the First Catholic Slovak Ladies Association (founded in Cleveland in 1892), the Slovak Catholic Sokol (originated in 1905), and the Slovak Gymnastic Union Sokol of the USA (founded in 1896).

In addition, a number of Slovak umbrella organizations have been formed to unite Slovaks with similar interests and promote common causes, including as follows: the Slovak Catholic Federation (1911), the Slovak League of America (1907), and the Friends of Slovakia (2001). Pittsburgh is home to one of 10 honorary consulates formed by the U.S. State Department, and the Western Pennsylvania Slovak Cultural Association formed in 1997 to bring diverse authentic Slovak cultural programs to western Pennsylvania. Pittsburgh also has two Slovak folk-dancing groups—the Pittsburgh Slovakians and the Pittsburgh Area Slovaks—and two weekly Slovak radio programs—the Western Pennsylvania Slovak Radio Hour and the McKeesport Slovak Radio Hour.

This c. 1930s photograph shows typical houses in a Slovak neighborhood located in the steel mill town of Duquesne, just 12 miles south of Pittsburgh. A woman sits on the front porch of the middle house. (Cathy Schoderbek.)

Slovaks in cluster communities relied on neighbors for camaraderie, friendship, and support in times of tragedy. In this undated image, a group of unidentified Slovak women socializes on the porch. (Lisa A. Alzo.)

Some towns were without a doubt heavily populated with residents of Slovak descent. This 2006 street sign for Slovak Way in Bradenville, located in Westmoreland County, marks a place where many Slovaks once lived. (John Matviya.)

The Slovak Home, founded in 1926 in Monessen, served as a club for Slovak social gatherings in the town. (Regina Feryok.)

The Slovak Radio Hour, *Vasa Nasa Slovenska Radiova Hodina*, on WHJB in 1938 featured live performances by local musicians. The show's host, Michael Sinchak (center), is pictured with one of the many bands that appeared live. Stanley Sinchak and Regina (Sinchak) Feryok appear in the background. (Teresa Sinchak.)

Members of a Slovak lodge who were also parishioners of Holy Name Roman Catholic Church in Monessen pose together for this undated photograph. (Regina Feryok.)

An inscribed plaque dated 1923 has been affixed to the bricks of the American Slovak Society Home. (John Matviya.)

This 2006 photograph depicts a monument from the American Slovak Society. It reads, "Dedicated to all the men and women who served our country in times of war and peace." The dedication was held on November 11, 1994. (John Matviya.)

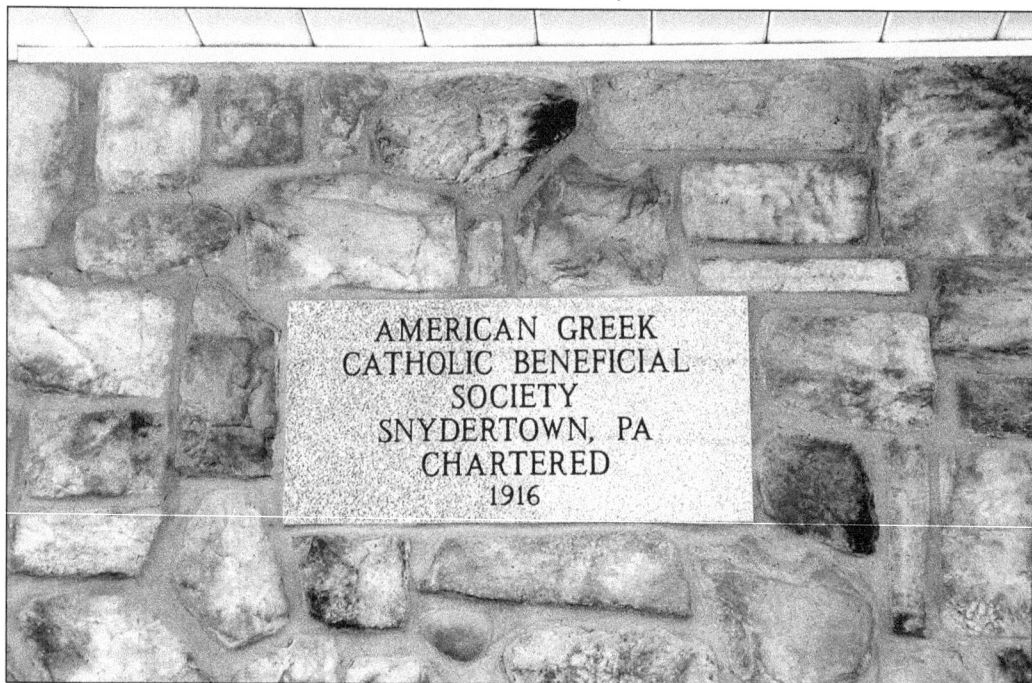

Fraternal benefit societies were founded in many towns throughout western Pennsylvania. Many even had their own buildings, such as the American Greek Catholic Beneficial Society in Snydertown, chartered in 1916. (John Matviya.)

In this undated photograph, Michael Sinchak (center) poses with a band that performed live on his Slovak Radio Hour on WHJB. Several youngsters participated in this particular band. (Teresa Sinchak.)

The Monessen Volunteer Fire Company Band entertains on Michael Sinchak's (first row, center) Slovak Radio Hour on WHJB around 1937. (Teresa Sinchak.)

Michael Sinchak (center) and John Hromey (right) pose with a third unidentified male at the Slovak Catholic Gymnastics Sokol in Monessen in the 1930s. The Slovak Gymnastics Sokol of the USA began in Bridgeport, Connecticut, in 1896. (Regina Feryok.)

Members of a dramatic club gather for a photograph in Monessen. (Sabra Clark.)

Community or fraternal baseball and softball teams provided another way for Slovaks to socialize. In this undated photograph, an unidentified team poses for the camera. (Cathy Schoderbek.)

For many sons of Slovak immigrants, sports provided for easier assimilation into American culture than work or other areas of life. This photograph shows the 1938 football team of Duquesne High School. (Lisa A. Alzo.)

Local Slovak sports heroes who were stars in high school went on to play for college teams. Joseph Figlar, seen in this undated photograph, was a football standout at Duquesne High School before going on to play for Case Western Reserve University. He then began a career as a high school football and wrestling coach at St. Edward's High School in Lakewood, Ohio. Figlar, like many Slovak men of the second generation, found his ticket to higher education through sports, earning a football scholarship. (Lisa A. Alzo.)

Many Slovak athletes, like John Alzo, excelled at sports such as basketball. This sports trading card was created in his honor in 2003 for permanent display at the Senator John Heinz Regional History Center in Pittsburgh. (Lisa A. Alzo.)

For many centuries, Slovakia and the Czech lands were part of the Austro-Hungarian Empire. The Pittsburgh Agreement, pictured here, was signed on May 31, 1918, to establish Czechoslovakia as a nation following World War I. In 1915, leaders of both the Slovaks and Czechs in America met to discuss a joint program for unification of their homelands. Prof. Thomas Masaryk, whose father was a native Slovak, and young Slovak leader Milan Stefanik began lobbying in Western Europe and in America for Slovak and Czech freedom. As a result, the Czecho-Slovak National Council was established in Paris in 1916, headed by Masaryk, Stefanik, and Edward Benes. This attempt at unification and separation from the Austro-Hungarian Empire was further enhanced by Pres. Woodrow Wilson's statement in 1917 that named the "Czecho-Slovaks" as one of the groups to be liberated. On May 31, 1918, during Masaryk's visit to Pittsburgh, the Pittsburgh Agreement was drafted and signed by representatives of the Slovak and Czech fraternal organizations in the United States. Over 25,000 Slovaks and Czechs gathered to support and proclaim publicly the desire to establish one country: Czechoslovakia. On October 27, Vienna accepted President Wilson's terms, thus officially proclaiming the national independence of Czechoslovakia on October 28, 1918. (Joseph Senko.)

In 1938, Michael Sinchak (right), along with a group of fellow Slovaks, traveled to Washington, D.C., to meet with Pres. Franklin D. Roosevelt. (Teresa Sinchak.)

A large number of Slovaks went through the naturalization process to become American citizens. This picture shows the men and women who were members of the class of 1928 Americanization School held at the United States Steel Works in Duquesne. (Cathy Schoderbek.)

Nine

FOOD, FOLKLORE, AND TRADITION

By living in cluster communities, Slovaks were able to continue the customs and traditions of their homeland. As for their diets, Slovak immigrants changed them only slightly upon arrival. In Slovakia, they had eaten a simple diet of potatoes, cheeses, milk, sauerkraut, and thick vegetable soups with vinegar or sour cream. Many similarities were found in the foods of all the Slavic peoples because of their common heritage. However, each nationality adhered to national or provincial tastes, which were reflected in variations in certain foods and unique methods of preparation. Recipes and cooking styles were often based on what foods were readily available and were also influenced by regional or local customs and practices. For Slovaks, it was not uncommon for their diet to remain unaltered for many years. Once the second generation tired of preparing traditional recipes, changes in diet began to take place. The children embraced American foods such as macaroni and cheese, hamburgers, ice cream, candy, and soda pop.

In the Slovak culture, food is richly entwined with tradition and religious teachings, especially for Christmas and Easter, when special dishes are prepared and rituals observed. Food is also used to establish a sense of community, and Slovaks have generally become known for their generosity and hospitality.

Slovaks carried out numerous rituals, which they believed foretold their future (especially prevalent during the Christmas season). Some rituals predicted the forthcoming year. For example, on November 30 (which began the Christmas season), they poured lead into boiling water and made predictions based on the shape of the cooled droplets. On Christmas Eve, Slovaks cracked nuts and used the condition of the meat as an indicator of what the upcoming year might hold for them, or the head of the household gave food from the dinner table to the family's animals in the hope of ensuring the livestock's health. Young women also had rituals that they believed might reveal the identities of their husbands.

The knowledge of local folk remedies was carried to the New World. For colds, Slovaks would grease the sick person with goose fat and put them to bed. For sore throats, they would fry garlic in goose lard and then add milk to make a drink, or mix up another concoction of whiskey, honey, and garlic. Pneumonia and diphtheria were treated by drinking kerosene with sugar in it, or straight whiskey.

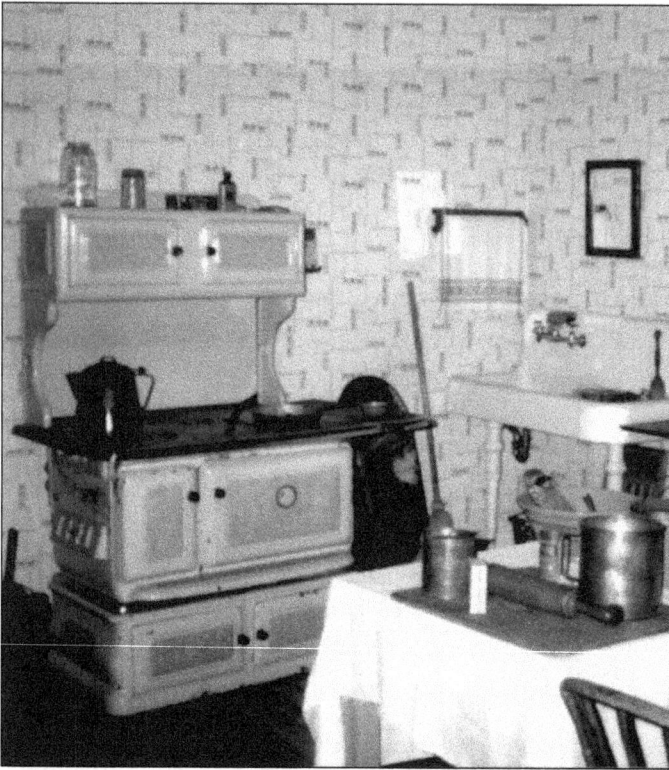

Whatever the occasion, the Slovak *Baba's* (grandmother's) kitchen functioned as the center of her home. It was where the Slovak woman spent the majority of her days as wife, mother, and grandmother, preserving the traditions of her homeland. There, in her domain, she also assumed the other important roles of comforter, teacher, disciplinarian, financial manager, and instiller of religious teachings, morals, and values. The kitchen also became the place where some of life's most important lessons were taught and learned. (Lisa A. Alzo.)

Dressed in an apron over a blue-and-white cotton house dress and with a babushka covering her hair, Veronica Figlar kneads dough for her mouth-watering golden buns, while her grandchildren look on with curiosity and anticipation. (Luanne Francesangeli.)

Slovak women were often noted for being wonderful cooks. In this July 1954 photograph, Mary Zavacky (left) and Anna Alzo prepare the dough required for baking Slovak cold dough cookies for an upcoming family wedding. (Lisa A. Alzo.)

Anna Alzo concentrates on cutting squares of dough at "just the right size" for a batch of *pirohi* during the 1990s. (Lisa A. Alzo.)

For Slovaks, holidays are typically bursting with tradition and often centered around the preparation of favorite foods. A traditional food for Slovaks is *pirohi* or *pirohy*—dough pockets filled with sauerkraut, potatoes, sweet cabbage, prunes, or dry cottage cheese. This dish is a classic favorite and a special part of family Christmas Eve gatherings. In this 2003 photograph, Gerry Abbott demonstrates the technique of dropping prepared *pirohi* into a pot of boiling water on the stove. (Lisa A. Alzo.)

On Christmas Eve, Slovaks celebrated with a meatless *Vilia* supper (to honor the Christian practice of fasting). During this supper, they ate foods like *bobalky*—perfectly baked little balls of dough browned in butter and mixed with sauerkraut, or in a poppy seed sauce—a special mushroom soup, and *pirohi*. (Lisa A. Alzo.)

In this 1928 photograph, Michael Sinchak (center background) and friends carry out a Christmas Slovak tradition: the *Jaslickari*, or "Bethlehem Strollers." Males both young and old would visit neighborhood homes dressed in costume, bringing Christmas greetings and singing carols. One of the males played the role of the *Kuba*, or clown, acting in a comical fashion. They would sometimes carry *klobassy* (sausage), saying it was a gift for the baby Jesus. It was customary for neighbors to offer alcoholic beverages to the *Jaslickari* following their caroling and long speeches that wished for health, happiness, and good fortune for the family. (Teresa Sinchak.)

At Easter, foods were served such as the *paska*, shown here. *Paska* is round bread with a golden crust and yellow center made from eggs, butter, and white raisins (indicative of living bread come down from Heaven). Slovaks typically ate this bread with other traditional Easter specialties such as *hrudka*, (also called *syrek*)—a bland, sweet, custard-like "cheese" made from cooked and separated eggs and milk (as a symbol of moderation)—ham, *klobassy*, and *chren/hrin*, which is a dish of beets mixed with horseradish. (Helen Lizanov.)

Slovaks took great pride in their food preparations. During Easter, the coloring and decorating of *pisanky* was an elaborate process. These eggs were placed along with the other traditional Easter foods in a large basket, covered with a special cloth, and taken to church on Holy Saturday to be blessed before the family would partake. (Cathy Schoderbek.)

Slovaks were gracious hosts. When a guest came to the home, inevitably a bottle of *slivovica/slivovitz* (plum brandy) would be placed on the table alongside two shot glasses. The toast *Na zdravie* or *nazdravye*, "To [your] health!," was pronounced before the guest and host would drink the brandy. (Lisa A. Alzo.)

Not all family traditions create fond memories. In this 1973 photograph, Lisa Alzo wears a wrap of cooked sauerkraut around her neck while suffering from the mumps as a child. This home remedy was passed on by Lisa's grandmother. (Lisa A. Alzo.)

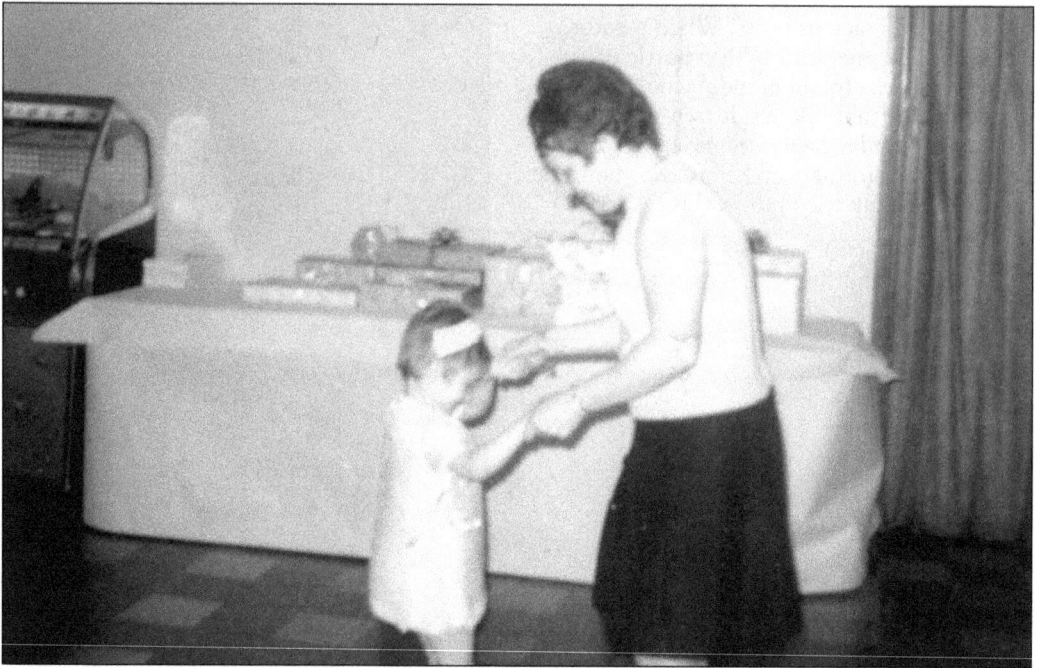

Anna Alzo teaches her daughter Lisa to dance a traditional Slovak polka at a family wedding held at the Slovak Civic Federation club in Duquesne in 1969. (Lisa A. Alzo.)

Musician John Hatala plays a lively Slovak tune on his accordion in this undated photograph. (Cathy Schoderbek.)

During traditional Slovak wedding receptions, the highlight of the evening was usually the bridal dance (*redovy*), during which the bride danced with male guests for a fee. This evolved from the Eastern European custom that required a bride's dance partners to contribute to her dowry. It was typically the last dance of the wedding after another ritual: the capping ceremony. There was an old Slovak myth that hair was magical and had to be concealed once married. In Slovakia, the bride's wreath or crown was ceremoniously removed by the village matron and replaced with a white, starched *cepec* (cap or kerchief) to be worn at all times. The cap served as a symbol that the woman was married and no longer available for courting. Slovaks in America adapted this to a removal of the bride's veil. While traditional music played, any man wishing to dance with the bride put money in a hat on the floor. The man then received a drink of whiskey. Here Geraldine (Figlar) Abbott, wearing a white kerchief on her head, dances with her brother Michael in 1962. (Lisa A. Alzo.)

Traditions kept alive through the generations act as a glue to bind people to their ancestors. Here Kimberly Augenstein Amey dances with her godfather, Michael Figlar, during a traditional Slovak *redovy* (bridal dance). She is wearing a traditional Slovak bridal cap from her maternal grandfather's village of Osturna. (Laurel Figlar.)

117

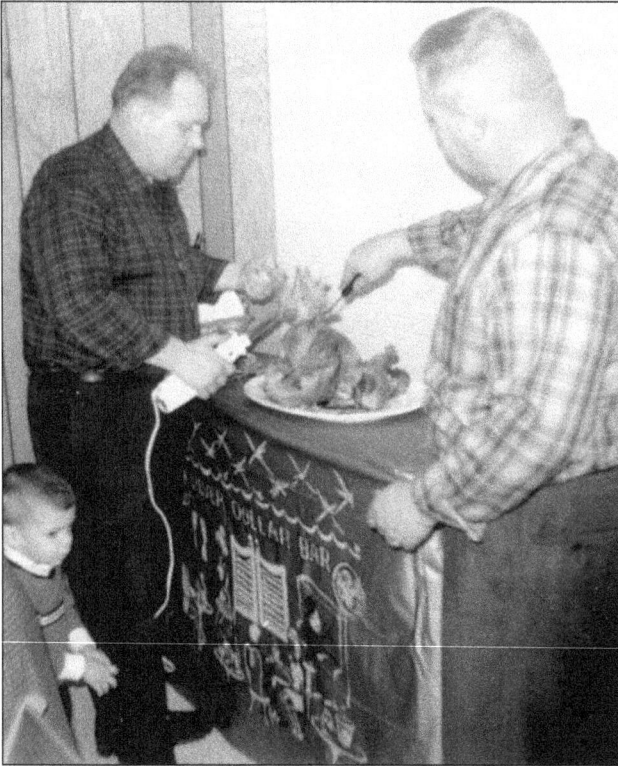

American holidays such as Thanksgiving, complete with turkey and all the trimmings, were celebrated in many Slovak homes. In this undated photograph, John (left) and Joe Figlar carve the turkey for their family's dinner. (Lisa A. Alzo.)

As Slovaks assimilated into American culture, they also adopted the ways of their local communities. In Pittsburgh, this meant cheering for the local professional sports teams, including the Pittsburgh Steelers, who have won five National Football League Super Bowl titles. In this late-1970s photograph, Veronica Figlar shows her team spirit in her black-and-gold Steeler's hat and scarf. (Lisa A. Alzo.)

Ten

CELEBRATIONS, EVENTS, AND FESTIVALS

In the old country, the social life of Slovaks almost always involved their neighbors. Once in America, the immigrants tried to have a similar type of social life, but the hours both men and women spent working made socializing somewhat of a luxury. For men, the main outlet was the neighborhood bar or tavern. Local ethnic clubs, sports teams, and fraternal lodges also provided opportunities for social interaction. For women, the church was the typical place to meet; however, Slovak women eventually rebelled from the male-dominated social organizations and founded their own societies.

Although Slovaks adjusted to American society, they preserved many of their customs and traditions involving food, folk dress, dance, and music. At interethnic or Slovak events, men, women, and children could often be seen in their *kroje* (traditional ethnic or peasant costumes). Items such as full skirts, puffed-sleeved blouses, shirts, trousers, aprons, bonnets and head scarves made from homespun cloth, and sheepskin hats or boots were easily identified by the multicolored and intricate embroidery. Specific styles, colors, and items included in the attire varied from region to region and could be so distinctive that they would simultaneously indicate a person's village and religion.

When attending the fraternal lodge or saloon or special occasion like a wedding, Slovaks enjoyed the traditional folk music played by local bands to which they danced the waltzes, *czardas*, and polkas.

The First Catholic Slovak Laymen's Retreat was held at the St. Andrew's Abbey in Cleveland June 25–28, 1936, with a number of Slovaks from Pittsburgh in attendance. (Mifflin Township Historical Society.)

SLOVAK CIVIC FEDERATION

Corner Fourth and Priscilla

Duquesne, Pa.

Twenty-Fifth

Anniversary

Banquet Celebration

SUNDAY EVENING, MAY 16, 1965

6:00 P.M.

The Slovak Civic Federation of Duquesne was founded by George L. Vesonder on December 12, 1937. With the encouragement and help of two other friends, many other Slovaks of Duquesne were contacted to meet at Vesonder's home to form and identify the organization. Vesonder declared, "Since other nationalists of Duquesne had organizations functioning and what an advantage such an organization would be to the Slovak people of Duquesne in the City's civic life, there certainly wasn't any reason why the Duquesne Slovaks could not form an organization." The program for the club's 25th anniversary celebration is shown here. Similar clubs formed in many other cities and towns throughout the Pittsburgh area. (Lisa A. Alzo.)

Smiling Slovaks pose in front of their first-place float at the Monessen Golden Jubilee in this 1948 photograph by Louis Studio. (Regina Feryok.)

Since 1924, on the third Thursday in July, thousands of people of all ages have gathered at Kennywood Amusement Park in West Mifflin to celebrate Slovak Day, one of several specially designated Nationality Days, which bring together Americans whose ancestors emigrated from around the world. This c. 1935 photograph shows happy attendees in ethnic costume at the entrance of the park. (Regina Feryok.)

Michael Sinchak (center) poses with two smiling, well-dressed ladies during Slovak Day at Kennywood Park about 1934. (Teresa Sinchak.)

This collage of photographs from previous Slovak Day celebrations at Kennywood Park shows several examples of the day's festivities. Above, several Roman Catholic priests preside over a mass in the pavilion. The center and lower photographs depict the happy faces of the volunteers who prepared the tasty Slovak foods featured in the *Slovenská Kuchyna* (Slovak Kitchen). (Western Pennsylvania Slovak Day Committee.)

Slovaks enjoyed many types of group gatherings such as ethnic picnics. In Bradenville, the American Slovak Society even had its own special picnic area, designated with the sign shown in this 2003 photograph. The sign would bear the name of the picnic being held on a particular day. (Lisa A. Alzo.)

In 1997, Slovak honorary consul Joseph T. Senko formed the nonprofit Western Pennsylvania Slovak Cultural Association (WPSCA) to bring diverse, authentic Slovak cultural programs to western Pennsylvania. Many of the programs sponsored by this group include talent from Slovakia. Another activity of the WPSCA is to honor those who by their distinguished leadership and service have enriched the Slovak culture and heritage at a testimonial awards dinner. Joseph Senko (left) is pictured with the 2004 Slovak Achievement Award recipient for education, Prof. Martin Votruba, a faculty member from the Department of Slavic Languages and Literatures at the University of Pittsburgh. (Joseph Senko.)

A group of smiling Slovaks from Monessen is about to embark on a tour of Czechoslovakia aboard the MN *Saturnia* in May 1952. (Regina Feryok.)

In preparation for the Christmas season each year, volunteers gather to decorate the Christmas tree at the Czechoslovak Nationality Classroom at the University of Pittsburgh's Cathedral of Learning in Oakland. The unique Nationality Classrooms in the university's 42-story Cathedral of Learning are gifts from the city's ethnic populations and serve as tributes to the multicultural heritage of Pittsburgh. All of these functioning classrooms are of museum quality and were designed by architects from abroad to re-create cultural periods prior to 1787, the founding date of the University of Pittsburgh. The Czechoslovak room was completed in 1939. The ceiling is a hand-carved and painted replica of a typical mountain villa in the Tatra region. Flowers indigenous to the Tatras are painted on the beams. Frescoes on the walls depict famous historical and literary Slovaks, including Jan Kollar, Bishop Moyzers, Ludovik Stur, and SS. Cyrill and Methodius. The room contains copies of artifacts representing the Czech and Slovak regions, as well as an original signed copy of the Pittsburgh Agreement. (Joseph Bielecki.)

Albina Senko poses with an unidentified Slovak friend in costume at a 2004 Christmas event held at the Mount Lebanon Library. (Albina Senko.)

Fifteenth Annual

Slovak

Heritage Festival

Sunday, November 6th, 2005
Cathedral of Learning
Commons Room

UNIVERSITY OF PITTSBURGH
SLOVAK STUDIES PROGRAM

Starting in 1990, on the first Sunday in November, the Slovak Student Club at the University of Pittsburgh sponsors an annual event at the Cathedral of Learning in Oakland. A large crowd can usually be seen enjoying Slovak musical and dance performances, viewing attractive displays, attending informative lectures, and purchasing authentic Slovak food items and artifacts from numerous vendors. (University of Pittsburgh Slovak Studies Program.)

The Pittsburgh Slovakians started in 1956 as one of two Slovak folk-dancing groups in the city (the other being the Pittsburgh Area Slovaks). Shown in this 2006 photograph, the Pittsburgh Slovakians group includes 32 singers and dancers who make approximately 25 public appearances each year. (Western Pennsylvania Slovak Day Committee.)

Every Memorial Day weekend, over 20 nationalities gather at a central location for the Pittsburgh Folk Festival. There they perform ethnic music and dances, sell ethnic food, and display cultural exhibits and folk crafts. Pittsburgh's Slovaks are always well represented at this popular festival, as evidenced by this 2006 display. (Lisa A. Alzo.)

Author and lecturer Lisa A. Alzo shows her Slovak pride by displaying her books about Slovak genealogy and immigration during the 50th Annual Pittsburgh Folk Festival at the David L. Lawrence Convention Center in Pittsburgh in May 2006. (Joyce Candi Grove.)

Visit us at
arcadiapublishing.com

www.ingramcontent.com/pod-product-compliance
Lightning Source LLC
Chambersburg PA
CBHW050554110426
42813CB00008B/2356